Psychology and Achievement

by Warren Hilton

PREFATORY NOTE

Lest in the text of these volumes credit may not always have been given where credit is due, grateful acknowledgment is here made to Professor Hugo Munsterberg, Professor Walter Dill Scott, Dr. James H. Hyslop, Dr. Ernst Haeckel, Dr. Frank Channing Haddock, Mr. Frederick W. Taylor, Professor Morton Prince, Professor F.H. Gerrish, Mr. Waldo Pondray Warren, Dr. J.D. Quackenbos, Professor C.A. Strong, Professor Paul Dubois, Professor Joseph Jastrow, Professor Pierre Janet, Dr. Bernard Hart and Professor G.M. Whipple, of the indebtedness to them incurred in the preparation of this work.

CONTENTS

ATTAINMENT OF MIND CONTROL

CHAPTER I

ATTAINMENT OF MIND CONTROL

[Sidenote: The Man of Tomorrow]

The men of the nineteenth century have harnessed the forces of the outer world. The age is now at hand that shall harness the energies of mind, new-found in the psychological laboratory, and shall put them at the service of humanity.

Are you fully equipped to take a valiant part in the work of the coming years?

[Sidenote: The Dollars and Cents of Mental Waste]

The greatest of all eras is at hand! Are you increasing your fitness to appreciate it and take part in it, or are you merely passing your time away?

Take careful note for a week of the incidents of your daily life--your methods of work, habits of thought, modes of recreation. You will discover an appalling waste in your present random methods of operation.

How many foot-pounds of energy do you suppose you annually dump into the scrap-heap of wasted effort? What does this mean to you in dollars and cents? In conscious usefulness? In peace and happiness?

[Sidenote: The Means to Notable Achievement]

Individual mental efficiency is an absolute prerequisite to any notable personal achievement or any great individual success. Your mental energies are the forces with which you must wage your battles in this world. Are you prepared to direct and deploy Achievement these forces with masterful control and strategic skill? Are you prepared to use all your reserves of mental energy in the crises of your career?

A Mighty and Intelligent Power resides within you. Its marvelous resources are just now coming to be recognized.

Recent scientific research has revealed, beyond the world of the senses and beyond the domain of consciousness, a wide and hitherto hidden realm of human energies and resources.

[Sidenote: A Process for "Making Good"]

These are mental energies and resources. They are phases of the mind, not of the "mind" of fifty years ago, but of a "mind" of whose operations you are unconscious and whose marvelous breadth and depth and power have but recently been revealed to the world by scientific experiment.

In this Basic Course of Reading we shall lay before you in simple and clear-cut but scientific form the proof that you have at your command mental powers of which you have never before dreamed.

And we shall give you such specific directions for the use of these new-found powers, that whatever your environment, whatever your business, whatever your ambition, you need but follow our plain and simple instructions in order to do the thing you want to do, to be the man you want to be, or to get the thing you want to have.

[Sidenote: Inadequacy of Body Training]

If you have any thought that the control of your hidden mental energies is to be acquired by mere hygienic measures, put it from you. The idea that you may come into the fulness of your powers through mere wholesome living, outdoor sports and bodily exercise is an idea that belongs to an age that is past. Good health is not necessary to achievement. It is not even a positive influence for achievement. It is merely a negative blessing. With good health you may hope to reach your highest mental and spiritual development free from the harassment of soul-racking pain. But without good health men have reached the summit of Parnassus and have dragged their tortured bodies up behind them.

[Sidenote: Inadequacy of Business Specialization]

Nor does success necessarily follow or require long preparation in a particular field. The first occupation of the successful man is rarely the one in which he achieves his ultimate triumph. In the changing conditions of our day, one needs a better weapon than the mere knowledge of a particular trade, vocation or profession. He needs that mastery of himself and others that is the fundamental secret of success in all fields of endeavor.

[Sidenote: Futility of Advice in Business]

It is well to tell you beforehand that in this Basic Course of Reading we shall be content with no mere cataloguing of the factors that are commonly regarded as essential to success. We shall do no moralizing. You will find here no elaboration of the ancient aphorisms, "Honesty is the best policy," and "Genius is the infinite capacity for taking pains."

The world has had its fill of mere exhortations to industry, frugality and perseverance. For some thousands of years men have preached to the lazy man, "Be industrious," and to the timid man, "Be bold." But such phrases never have solved and never can solve the problem for the man who feels himself lacking in both industry and courage.

[Sidenote: The Why and the How]

It is easy enough to tell the salesman that he must approach his "prospect" with tact and confidence. But tact and confidence are not qualities that can be assumed and discarded like a Sunday coat. Industry and courage and tact and confidence are well enough, but we must know the Why and the How of these things.

It is well enough to preach that the secret of achievement is to be found in "courage-faith" and "courage-confidence," and that the way to acquire these qualities is to assume that you have them. There is no denying the undoubted fact that men and women have been rescued from the deepest mire of poverty and despair and lifted to planes of happy abundance by what is known as "faith." But what is "faith"? And "faith" in What? And Why? And How?

[Sidenote: Fundamental Training for Efficiency]

Obviously we cannot achieve certain and definite results in this or any other field so long as we continue to deal with materials we do not understand. Yet that is what all men are doing today. The elements of truth are befogged in vague and amateurish mysticism, and the subject of individual efficiency when we get beyond mere preaching and moralizing is a chaos of isms.

The time is ripe for a real analysis of these important problems,--a serious and scientific analysis with a clear and practical exposition of facts and principles and rules for conduct.

Men and women must be fundamentally trained so that they can look deep into their own minds and see where the screw is loose, where oil is needed, and so readjust themselves and their living for a greater efficiency.

[Sidenote: The Virus of Failure]

The embittered, the superstitious, the prejudiced, all those who scorpion-like sting themselves with the virus of failure, must be given an antidote of understanding that will repair their deranged mental machinery.

The conscientious but foolish business man who is worrying himself into failure and an early grave must be taught the physiological effects of ideas and given a new standard of values.

The profligate must be lured from his emotional excesses and debaucheries, not by moralizings, but by showing him just how these things fritter his energies and retard his progress.

[Sidenote: Practical Formulas for Every Day]

It must be made plain to the successful promoter, to the rich banker, how a man may be a financial success and yet a miserable failure so far as true happiness is concerned, and how by scientific self-development he can acquire greater riches within than all his vaults of steel will hold.

This Basic Course of Reading offers just such an analysis and exposition of fundamental principles. It furnishes definite and scientific answers to the problems of life. It will reveal to you unused or unintelligently used mental forces vastly greater than those now at your command.

[Sidenote: Your Undiscovered Resources]

We go even further, and say that this Basic Course of Reading provides a practicable formula for the everyday use of these vast resources. It will enable you to acquire the magical qualities and still more magical effects that spell success and happiness, without straining your will to the breaking point and making life a burden. It will give you a definite prescription like the physician's, "Take one before meals," and as easily compounded, which will enable you to be prosperous and happy.

In the development of one's innate resources, such as powers of observation, imagination, correct judgment, alertness, resourcefulness, application, concentration, and the faculty of taking prompt advantage of opportunities, the study of the mental machine is bound to be the first step. It must be the ultimate resource for self-training in efficiency for the promoter with his appeal to the cupidity and imaginations of men as surely as for the artist in his search for poetic inspiration.

[Sidenote: Man's Mind Machine]

No man can get the best results from any machine unless he understands its mechanism. We shall draw aside the curtain and show you the mind in operation.

The mastery of your own powers is worth more to you than all the knowledge of outside facts you can crowd into your head. Read and study and practice the teachings of this Basic Course, and they will make you in a new sense the master of yourself and of your future.

In this Basic Course of Reading we shall begin by giving you a thorough understanding of certain mental operations and processes.

[Sidenote: Abjuring Mysticisms]

We shall lead your interest away from "vague mysticisms" and emphasize such phases of scientific psychological theory as bear directly on practical achievement.

We shall give you a practical working knowledge of concentrative mental methods and devices. We shall clear away the mysteries and misapprehensions that now envelop this particular field.

In the present volume we shall begin with a discussion of certain aspects of the relation between the mind and the body.

[Sidenote: Psychology, Physiology and Relationships]

However we look at it, it is impossible to understand the mind without some knowledge of the bodily machine through which the mind works. The investigation of the mind and its conditions and problems is primarily the business of psychology, which seeks to describe and explain them. It would seem to be entirely distinct from physiology, which seeks to classify and explain the facts of bodily structure and operation. But all sciences overlap more or less. And this is particularly true of psychology, which deals with the mind, and physiology, which deals with the body.

It is the mind that we are primarily interested in. But every individual mind resides within, or at least expresses itself through, a body. Upon the preservation of that body and upon the orderly performance of its functions depend our health and comfort, our very lives.

[Sidenote: Abode and instrument of Mind]

Then, too, considered merely as part of the outside world of matter, man's body is the physical fact with which he is most in contact and most immediately concerned. It furnishes him with information concerning the existence and operations of other minds. It is in fact his only source of information about the outside world.

First of all, then, you must form definite and intelligent conclusions concerning the relations between the mind and the body.

[Sidenote: Manner of Handling Mental Processes]

This will be of value in a number of ways. In the first place, you will understand the bodily mechanism through which the mind operates, and a knowledge of this mechanism is bound to enlighten you as to the character of the mental processes themselves. In the second place, it is worth while to know the extent of the mind's influence over the body, because this knowledge is the first step toward obtaining bodily efficiency through the mental control of bodily functions. And, finally, a study of this bodily mechanism is of very great practical importance in itself, for the body is the instrument through which the mind acts in its relations with the world at large.

From a study of the bodily machine, we shall advance to a consideration of the mental processes themselves, not after the usual manner of works on psychology, but solely from the standpoint of practical utility and for the establishment of a scientific concept of the mind capable of everyday use.

[Sidenote: Fundamental Laws and Practical Methods]

The elucidation of every principle of mental operation will be accompanied by illustrative material pointing out just how that particular law may be employed for the attainment of specific practical ends. There will be numerous illustrative instances and methods that can be at once made use of by the merchant, the musician, the salesman, the advertiser, the employer of labor, the business executive.

[Sidenote: Special Business Topics]

In this way this Basic Course of Reading will lay a firm and broad foundation, first, for an understanding of the methods and devices whereby any man may acquire full control and direction of his mental energies and may develop his resources to the last degree; second, for an understanding of the psychological methods for success in any specific professional pursuit in which he may be particularly interested; and third, for an understanding of the methods of applying psychological knowledge to the industrial problems of office, store and factory.

The first of these--that is to say, instruction in methods for the attainment of any goal consistent with native ability--will follow right along as part of this Basic Course of Reading. The second and third--that is to say, the study of special commercial and industrial topics--are made the subject of special courses supplemental to this Basic Course and for which it can serve only as an introduction.

[Sidenote: A Step Beyond Collegiate Psychology]

In this Basic Course of Reading we shall show you how you may acquire perfect individual efficiency. And, most remarkable of all, we shall show you how you may acquire it without that effort to obtain it, that straining of the will, that struggling with wasteful inclinations and desires, that is itself the essence of inefficiency.

The facts and principles set forth in this Basic Course are new and wonderful and inspiring. They have been established and attested by world-wide and exhaustive scientific research and experiment.

[Sidenote: The Eternal Laws of Individual Achievement]

You may be a college graduate. You may have had the advantage of a college course in psychology. But you have probably had no instruction in the practical application of your knowledge of mental operations. So far as we are aware, there are few universities in the world that embrace in their curricula a course in "applied" psychology. For the average college man this Basic Course of Reading will be, therefore, in the nature of a post-graduate course, teaching him how to make practical use of the psychology he learned at college, and in addition giving him facts about the mind unknown to the college psychology of a few years ago.

In these books you will probe deeply into the normal human mind.

You will see also the fantastic and distorted shape of its manifestations in disease.

You will learn the Eternal Laws of Individual Achievement.

[Sidenote: How to Master Our Methods]

And you will be taught how to apply them to your own business or profession.

But mark this word of warning. To comprehend the teachings of this Basic Course well enough to put them into practice demands from you careful study and reflection. It requires persistent application. Do not attempt to browse through the pages that follow. They are worth all the time that you can put upon them.

The mind is a complex mechanism. Each element is alone a fitting subject for a lifetime's study. Do not lose sight of the whole in the study of the parts.

All the books bear upon a central theme. They will lead you on step by step. Gradually your conception of your relations to the world will change. A new realization of power will come upon you. You will learn that you are in a new sense the master of your fate. You will find these books, like the petals of a flower, unfolding one by one until a great and vital truth stands revealed in full-blown beauty.

To derive full benefit from the Course it is necessary that you should do more than merely understand each sentence as you go along. You must grasp the underlying train of thought. You must perceive the continuity of the argument.

It is necessary, therefore, that you do but a limited amount of reading each day, taking ample time to reflect on what you have read. If any book is not entirely clear to you at first, go over it again. Persistence will enable any man to acquire a thorough comprehension of our teachings and a profound mastery of our methods.

TWO LAWS OF SUCCESS-ACHIEVEMENT

CHAPTER II

TWO LAWS OF SUCCESS-ACHIEVEMENT

[Sidenote: The One-Man Business Corporation]

As a working unit you are a kind of one-man business corporation made up of two departments, the mental and the physical.

Your mind is the executive office of this personal corporation, its directing "head." Your body is the corporation's "plant." Eyes and ears, sight and smell and touch, hands and feet--these are the implements, the equipment.

We have undertaken to teach you how to acquire a perfect mastery of your own powers and meet the practical problems of your life in such a way that success will be swift and certain.

[Sidenote: Business and Bodily Activity]

First of all it is necessary that you should accept and believe two well-settled and fundamental laws.

I. All human achievement comes about through bodily activity.

II. All bodily activity is caused, controlled and directed by the mind.

Give the first of these propositions but a moment's thought. You can conceive of no form of accomplishment which is not the result of some kind of bodily activity. One would say that the master works of poetry, art, philosophy, religion, are products of human effort furthest removed from the material side of life, yet even these would have perished still-born in the minds conceiving them had they not found transmission and expression through some form of bodily activity. You will agree, therefore, that the first of these propositions is so self-evident, so axiomatic, as neither to require nor to admit of formal proof.

The second proposition is not so easily disposed of. It is in fact so difficult of acceptance by some persons that we must make very plain its absolute validity. Furthermore, its elucidation will bring forth many illuminating facts that will give you an entirely new conception of the mind and its scope and influence.

[Sidenote: The Enslaved Brain]

Remember, when we say "mind," we are not thinking of the brain. The brain is but one of the organs of the body, and, by the terms of our proposition as stated, is as much the slave of the mind as is any other organ of the body. To say that the mind controls the body presupposes that mind and body are distinct entities, the one belonging to a spiritual world, the other to a world of matter.

That the mind is master of the body is a settled principle of science. But we realize that its acceptance may require you to lay aside some preconceived prejudices. You may be one of those who believe that the mind is nothing more nor less than brain activity. You may believe that the body is all there is to man and that mind-action is merely one of its functions.

[Sidenote: First Step Toward Self-Realization]

If so, we want you nevertheless to realize that, while as a matter of philosophic speculation you retain these opinions, you may at the same time for practical purposes regard the mind as an independent causal agency and believe that it can and does control and determine and cause any and every kind of bodily activity. We want you to do this because this conclusion is at the basis of a practical system of mental efficiency and because, as we shall at once show you, it is capable of proof by the established methods of physical science.

RELATION OF MIND ACTIVITY TO BODILY ACTIVITY

CHAPTER III

RELATION OF MIND ACTIVITY TO BODILY ACTIVITY

POINT OF VIEW FROM WHICH YOU MUST APPROACH THIS PROBLEM

[Sidenote: Speculation and Practical Science]

The fact is, one's opinion as to whether mind controls body or body makes mind-action depends altogether upon the point of view. And the first step for us to take is to agree upon the point of view we shall assume.

Two points of view are possible. One is speculative, the other practical.

[Sidenote: Philosophic Riddles and Personal Effectiveness]

The speculative point of view is that of the philosopher and religionist, who ponder the tie that binds "soul" and body in an effort to solve the riddle of "creation" and pierce the mystery of the "hereafter."

The practical point of view is that of the modern practical scientist, who deals only with actual facts of human experience and seeks only immediate practical results.

The speculative problem is the historical and religious one of the mortality or immortality of the soul. The practical problem is the scientific one that demands to know what the mental forces are and how they can be used most effectively.

[Sidenote: What We Want to Know]

There is no especial need here to trace the historical development of these two problems or enter upon a discussion of religious or philosophical questions.

Our immediate interest in the mind and its relationship to the body is not because we want to be assured of the salvation of our souls after death.

We want to know all we can about the reality and certainty and character of mental control of bodily functions because of the practical use we can make of such knowledge in this life, here and now.

[Sidenote: Spiritualist, Materialist and Scientist]

The practical scientist has nothing in common with either spiritualists, soul-believers, on the one hand, or materialists on the other. So far as the mortality of the soul is concerned, he may be either a spiritualist or a materialist But spiritualism or materialism is to him only an intellectual pastime. It is not his trade. In his actual work he seeks only practical results, and so confines himself wholly to the actual facts of human experience.

The practical scientist knows that as between two given facts, and only as between these two, one may be the "cause" of the other. But he is not interested in the "creative origin" of material things. He does not attempt to discover "first" causes.

[Sidenote: Science of Cause and Effect]

The practical scientist ascribes all sorts of qualities to electricity and lays down many laws concerning it without having the remotest idea as to what, in the last analysis, electricity may actually be. He is not concerned with ultimate truths. He does his work, and necessarily so, upon the principle that for all practical purposes he is justified in using any given assumption as a working hypothesis if everything happens just as if it were true.

The practical scientist applies the term "cause" to any object or event that is the invariable predecessor of some other object or event.

For him a "cause" is simply any object or event that may be looked upon as forecasting the action of some other object or the occurrence of some other event.

The point with him is simply this, Does or does not this object or this event in any way affect that object or that event or determine its behavior?

[Sidenote: Causes and "First" Causes]

No matter where you look you will find that every fact in Nature is relatively cause and effect according to the point of view. Thus, if a railroad engine backs into a train of cars it transmits a certain amount of motion to the first car. This imparted motion is again passed on to the next car, and so on. The motion of the first car is, on the one hand, the effect of the impact of the engine, and is, on the other hand, the "cause" of the motion of the second car. And, in general, what is an "effect" in the first car becomes a "cause" when looked at in relation to the second, and what is an "effect" in the second becomes a "cause" in relation to the third. So that even the materialist will agree that "cause" and "effect" are relative terms in dealing with any series of facts in Nature.

[Sidenote: A Common Platform for All]

A man may be either a spiritualist, believing that the mind is a manifestation of the super-soul, or he may be a materialist, and in either case he may at the same time and with perfect consistency believe, as a practical scientist, that the mind is a "cause" and has bodily action as its "effect."

Naturally this point of view offers no difficulties whatever to the spiritualist. He already looks upon the mind or soul as the "originating cause" of everything.

[Sidenote: Thoughts Treated as Causes]

But the materialist, too, may in accordance with his speculative theory continue to insist that brain-action is the "originating cause" of mental life; yet if the facts show that certain thoughts are invariably followed by certain bodily activities, the materialist may without violence to his theories agree to the great practical value of treating these thoughts as immediate causes, no matter what the history of creation may have been.

Whatever the brand of your materialism or your religious belief, you can join us in accepting this practical-science point of view as a common platform upon which to approach our second fundamental proposition, that "all bodily activity is caused, controlled and directed by the mind."

[Sidenote: Scientific Method with Practical Problems]

Ignoring all religious and metaphysical questions, we have, then, to ask ourselves merely: Can the mind be relied upon to bring about or stop or in any manner influence bodily action? And if it can, what is the extent of the mind's influence?

In answering these questions we shall follow the method of the practical scientist, whose method is invariably the same whatever the problem he is investigating.

This method involves two steps: first, the collection and classification of facts; second, the deduction from those facts of general principles.

[Sidenote: Uses of Scientific Laws]

The scientist first gathers together the greatest possible array of experiential facts and classifies these facts into sequences--that is to say, he gathers together as many instances as he can find in which one given fact follows directly upon the happening of another given fact.

Having done this, he next formulates in broad general terms the common principle that he finds embodied in these many similar sequences.

Such a formula, if there are facts enough to establish it, is what is known as a scientific law. Its value to the world lies in this, that whenever the given fact shall again occur our knowledge of the scientific law will enable us to predict with certainty just what events will follow the occurrence of that fact.

First, then, let us marshal our facts tending to prove that bodily activities are caused by the mind.

INTROSPECTIVE EVIDENCE OF MENTAL MASTERY

CHAPTER IV

INTROSPECTIVE EVIDENCE OF MENTAL MASTERY

[Sidenote: Doing the Thing You Want to Do]

The first and most conspicuous evidential fact is voluntary bodily action; that is to say, bodily action resulting from the exercise of the conscious will.

[Sidenote: Source of Power of Will]

If you will a bodily movement and that movement immediately follows, you are certainly justified in concluding that your mind has caused the bodily movement. Every conscious, voluntary movement that you make, and you are making thousands of them every hour, is a distinct example of mind activity causing bodily action. In fact, the very will to make any bodily movement is itself nothing more nor less than a mental state.

The will to do a thing is simply the belief, the conviction, that the appropriate bodily movement is about to occur. The whole scientific world is agreed on this.

For example, in order to bend your forefinger do you first think it over, then deliberately put forth some special form of energy? Not at all: The very thought of bending the finger, if unhindered by conflicting ideas, is enough to bend it.

[Sidenote: Impellent Energy of Thought]

Note this general law: The idea of any bodily action tends to produce the action.

This conception of thought as impellent--that is to say, as impelling bodily activity--is of absolutely fundamental importance. The following simple experiments will illustrate its working.

Ask a number of persons to think successively of the letters "B," "O," and "Q." They are not to pronounce the letters, but simply to think hard about the sound of each letter.

[Sidenote: Bodily effects of Mental States]

Now, as they think of these letters, one after the other, watch closely and you will see their lips move in readiness to pronounce them. There may be some whose lip-movements you will be unable to detect. If so, it will be because your eye is not quick enough or keen enough to follow them in every case.

Have a friend blindfold you and then stand behind you with his hands on your shoulders. While in this position ask him to concentrate his mind upon some object in another part of the house. Yield yourself to the slightest pressure of his hands or arms and you will soon come to the object of which he has been thinking. If he is unfamiliar with the impelling energy of thought, he will charge the result to mind-reading.

[Sidenote: Illustrative Experiments]

The same law is illustrated by a familiar catch. Ask a friend to define the word "spiral." He will find it difficult to express the meaning in words. And nine persons out of ten while groping for appropriate words will unconsciously describe a spiral in the air with the forefinger.

Swing a locket in front of you, holding the end of the chain with both hands. You will soon see that it will swing in harmony with your thoughts. If you think of a circle, it will swing around in a circle. If you think of the movement of a pendulum, the locket will swing back and forth.

These experiments not only illustrate the impelling energy of thought and its power to induce bodily action, but they indicate also that the bodily effects of mental action are not limited to bodily movements that are conscious and voluntary.

[Sidenote: Scope of Mind Power]

The fact is, every mental state whether you consider it as involving an act of the will or not, is followed some kind of bodily effect, and every bodily action is preceded by some distinct kind of mental activity. From the practical science point of view every thought causes its particular bodily effects.

This is true of simple sensations. It is true of impulses, ideas and emotions. It is true of pleasures and pains. It is true of conscious mental activity. It is true of unconscious mental activity. It is true of the whole range of mental life.

Since the mental conditions that produce bodily effects are not limited to those mental conditions in which there is a conscious exercise of the will, it follows that the bodily effects produced by mental action are not limited to movements of what are known as the voluntary muscles.

On the contrary, they include changes and movements in all of the so-called involuntary muscles, and in every kind of bodily structure. They include changes and movements in every part of the physical organism, from changes in the action of heart, lungs, stomach, liver and other viscera, to changes in the secretions of glands and in the caliber of the tiniest blood-vessels. A few instances such as are familiar to the introspective experience of everyone will illustrate the scope of the mind's control over the body.

[Sidenote: Bodily Effects of Emotion]

Emotion always causes numerous and intense bodily effects. Furious anger may cause frowning brows, grinding teeth, contracted jaws, clenched fists, panting breath, growling cries, bright redness of the face or sudden paleness. None of these effects is voluntary; we may not even be conscious of them.

Fright may produce a wild beating of the heart, a death-like pallor, a gasping motion of the lips, an uncovering or protruding of the eye-balls, a sudden rigidity of the body as if "rooted" to the spot.

Grief may cause profuse secretion of tears, swollen, reddened face, red eyes and other familiar symptoms.

Shame may cause that sudden dilation of the capillary blood-vessels of the face known as "blushing."

[Sidenote: Bodily Effects of Perception]

The sight of others laughing or yawning makes us laugh or yawn. The sound of one man coughing will become epidemic in an audience. The thought of a sizzling porter-house steak with mushrooms, baked potatoes and rich gravy makes the mouth of a hungry man "water."

Suppose I show you a lemon cut in half and tell you with a wry face and puckered mouth that I am going to suck the juice of this exceedingly sour lemon. As you merely read these lines you may observe that the glands in your mouth have begun to secrete saliva. There is a story of a man who wagered with a friend that he could stop a band that was playing in front of his office. He got three lemons and gave half of a lemon to each of a number of street urchins. He then had these boys walk round and round the band, sucking the lemons and making puckered faces at the musicians. That soon ended the music.

[Sidenote: Experiments of Pavlov]

A distinguished German scientist, named Pavlov, has recently demonstrated in a series of experiments with dogs that the sight of the plate that ordinarily bears their food, or the sight of the chair upon which the plate ordinarily stands, or even the sight of the person who commonly brings the plate, may cause the saliva to flow from their salivary glands just as effectively as the food itself would do if placed in their mouths.

[Sidenote: Taste and digestion]

There was a time, and that not long ago, when the contact of food with the lining of the stomach was supposed to be the immediate cause of the secretion of the digestive fluids. Yet recent observation of the interior of the stomach through an incision in the body, has shown that just as soon as the food is tasted in the mouth, a purely mental process, the stomach begins to well forth those fluids that are suitable for digestion.

[Sidenote: Bodily Effects of Sensations]

The press recently contained an account of a motorcycle race in Newark, New Jersey. The scene was a great bowl-shaped motor-drome. In the midst of cheering thousands, when riding at the blinding speed of ninety-two miles an hour, the motorcycle of one of the contestants went wrong. It climbed the twenty-eight-foot incline, hurled its rider to instant death and crashed into the packed grandstand. Before the whirling mass of steel was halted by a deep-set iron pillar four men lay dead and twenty-two others unconscious and severely injured. Then the twisted engine of death rebounded from the post and rolled down the saucer-rim of the track.

Around the circular path, his speed scarcely less than that of his ill-fated rival, knowing nothing of the tragedy, hearing nothing of the screams of warning from the crowd, came another racer. The frightened throng saw the coming of a second tragedy. The sound that came from the crowd was a low moaning, a sighing, impotent, unconscious prayer of the thousands for the mercy that could not come. The second motorcycle struck the wreck, leaped into the air, and the body of its rider shot fifty feet over the handlebars and fell at the bottom of the track unconscious. Two hours later he was dead.

What was the effect of this dreadful spectacle upon the onlookers? Confusion, cries of fright and panic, while throughout the grandstand women fainted and lay here and there unconscious. Many were afflicted with nausea. With others the muscles of speech contracted convulsively, knees gave way, hearts "stopped beating." Observe that these were wholly the effects of mental action, effects of sight and sound sensations.

[Sidenote: The Fundamental Law of Expression]

Why multiply instances? All that you need to do to be satisfied that the mind is directly responsible for any and every kind of bodily activity is to examine your own experiences and those of your friends. They will afford you innumerable illustrations.

You will find that not only is your body constantly doing things because your mind wills that it should do them, but that your body is incessantly doing things simply because they are the expression of a passing thought.

The law that Every idea tends to express itself in some form of bodily activity, is one of the most obviously demonstrable principles of human life.

Bear in mind that this is but another way of expressing the second of our first two fundamental principles of mental efficiency, and that we are engaged in a scientific demonstration of its truth so that you will not confuse it with mere theory or speculation.

To recall these fundamental principles to your mind and further impress them upon you, we will restate them:

I. All human achievement comes about through some form of bodily activity.

II. All bodily activity is caused, controlled and directed by the mind.

PHYSIOLOGICAL EVIDENCE OF MENTAL MASTERY

CHAPTER V

PHYSIOLOGICAL EVIDENCE OF MENTAL MASTERY

[Sidenote: Introspective Knowledge]

We have been considering the relationship between mind and body from the standpoint of the mind. Our investigation has been largely introspective; that is to say, we simply looked within ourselves and considered the effects of our mental operations upon our own bodies. The facts we had before us were facts of which we had direct knowledge. We did not have to go out and seek them in the mental and bodily activities of other persons. We found them here within ourselves, inherent in our consciousness. To observe them we had merely to turn the spotlight into the hidden channels of our own minds.

[Sidenote: Dissection and the Governing Consciousness]

We come now to examine the mind's influence upon the body from the standpoint of the body. To do this we must go forth and investigate. We must use eye, ear and hand. We must use the forceps and scalpel and microscope of the anatomist and physiologist.

[Sidenote: Subordinate Mental Units]

But it is well worth while that we should do this. For our investigation will show a bodily structure peculiarly adapted to control by a governing consciousness. It will reveal to the eye a physical mechanism peculiarly fitted for the dissemination of intelligence throughout the body. And, most of all, it will disclose the existence within the body of subordinate mental units, each capable of receiving, understanding and acting upon the intelligence thus submitted. And we shall have strongly corroborative evidence of the mind's complete control over every function of the body.

Examine a green plant and you will observe that it is composed of numerous parts, each of which has some special function to perform. The roots absorb food and drink from the soil. The leaves breathe in carbonic acid from the air and transform it into the living substance of the plant. Every plant has, therefore, an anatomical structure, its parts and tissues visible to the naked eye.

[Sidenote: What the Microscope Shows]

Put one of these tissues under a microscope and you will find that it consists of a honeycomb of small compartments or units. These compartments are called "cells," and the structure of all plant tissues is described as "cellular." Wherever you may look in any plant, you will find these cells making up its tissues. The activity of any part or tissue of the plant, and consequently all of the activities of the plant as a whole, are but the combined and co-operating activities of the various individual cells of which the tissues are composed. The living cell, therefore, is at the basis of all plant life.

[Sidenote: The Little Universe Beyond]

In the same way, if you turn to the structure of any animal, you will find that it is composed of parts or organs made up of different kinds of tissues, and these tissues examined under a microscope will disclose a cellular structure similar to that exhibited by the plant.

Look where you will among living things, plant or animal, you will find that all are mere assemblages of cellular tissues.

Extend your investigation further, and examine into forms of life so minute that they can be seen only with the most powerful microscope and you will come upon a whole universe of tiny creatures consisting of a single cell.

[Sidenote: The Unit of Life]

Indeed, it is a demonstrable fact that these tiny units of life consisting of but a single cell are far more numerous than the forms of life visible to the naked eye. You will have some idea of their size and number when we tell you that millions may live and die and reproduce their kind in a single thimbleful of earth.

Every plant, then, or every animal, whatever its species, however simple or complicated its structure, is in the last analysis either a single cell or a confederated group of cells.

All life, whether it be the life of a single cell or of an unorganized group of cells or of a republic of cells, has as its basis the life of the cell.

For all the animate world, two great principles stand established. First, that every living organism, plant or animal, big or little, develops from a cell, and is itself a composite of cells, and that the cell is the unit of all life. Secondly, that the big and complex organisms have through long ages developed out of simpler forms, the organic life of today being the result of an age-long process of evolution.

What, then, is the cell, and what part has it played in this process of evolution?

To begin with, a cell is visible only through a microscope. A human blood cell is about one-three-thousandth of an inch across, while a bacterial cell may be no more than one-twenty-five-thousandth of an inch in diameter.

[Sidenote: Characteristics of Living Cells]

Yet, small as it is, the cell exhibits all of the customary phenomena of independent life; that is to say, it nourishes itself, it grows, it reproduces its kind, it moves about, and it feels. It is a living, breathing, feeling, moving, feeding thing.

The term "cell" suggests a walled-in enclosure. This is because it was originally supposed that a confining wall or membrane was an invariable and essential characteristic of cell structure. It is now known, however, that while such a membrane may exist, as it does in most plant cells, it may be lacking, as is the case in most animal cells.

The only absolutely essential parts of the cell are the inner nucleus or kernel and the tiny mass of living jelly surrounding it, called the protoplasm.

[Sidenote: The Brain of the Cell]

The most powerful microscopes disclose in this protoplasm a certain definite structure, a very fine, thread-like network spreading from the nucleus throughout the semi-fluid albuminous protoplasm. It is certainly in line with the broad analogies of life, to suppose that in each cell the nucleus with its network is the brain and nervous system of that individual cell.

All living organisms consist, then simply of cells. Those consisting of but one cell are termed unicellular; those comprising more than one cell are called pluricellular.

The unicellular organism is the unit of life on this earth. Yet tiny and ultimate as it is, every unicellular organism is possessed of an independent and "free living" existence.

[Sidenote: Mind Life of One Cell]

To be convinced of this fact, just consider for a moment the scope of development and range of activities of one of these tiny bodies.

"We see, then," says Haeckel, "that it performs all the essential life functions which the entire organism accomplishes. Every one of these little beings grows and feeds itself independently. It assimilates juices from without, absorbing them from the surrounding fluid. Each separate cell is also able to reproduce itself and to increase. This increase generally takes place by simple division, the nucleus parting first, by a contraction round its circumference, into two parts; after which the protoplasm likewise separates into two divisions. The single cell is able to move and creep about; from its outer surface it sends out and draws back again finger-like processes, thereby modifying its form. Finally, the young cell has feeling, and is more or less sensitive. It performs certain movements on the application of chemical and mechanical irritants."

[Sidenote: The Will of the Cell]

The single living cell moves about in search of food. When food is found it is enveloped in the mass of protoplasm, digested and assimilated.

The single cell has the power of choice, for it refuses to eat what is unwholesome and extends itself mightily to reach that which is nourishing.

[Sidenote: The Cell and Organic Evolution]

Moebius and Gates are convinced that the single cell possesses memory, for having once encountered anything dangerous, it knows enough to avoid it when presented under similar circumstances. And having once found food in a certain place, it will afterwards make a business of looking for it in the same place.

And, finally, Verwen and Binet have found in a single living cell manifestations of the emotions of surprise and fear and the rudiments of an ability to adapt means to an end.

Let us now consider pluricellular organisms and consider them particularly from the standpoint of organic evolution. The pluricellular organism is nothing more nor less than a later development, a confederated association of unicellular organisms. Mark the development of such an association.

[Sidenote: Evolutionary Differentiation]

Originally each separate cell performed all the functions of a separate life. The bonds that united it to its fellows were of the most transient character. Gradually the necessities of environment led to a more and more permanent grouping, until at last the bonds of union became indissoluble.

Meanwhile, the great laws of "adaptation" and "heredity," the basic principles of evolution, have been steadily at work, and slowly there has come about a differentiation of cell function, an apportionment among the different cells of the different kinds of labor.

[Sidenote: Plurality of the Individual]

As the result of such differentiation, the pluricellular organism, as it comes ultimately to be evolved, is composed of many different kinds of cells. Each has its special function. Each has its field of labor. Each lives its own individual life. Each reproduces its own kind. Yet all are bound together as elements of the same "cell society" or organized "cell state."

Among pluricellular organisms man is of course supreme. He is the one form of animal life that is most highly differentiated.

[Sidenote: Combined Consciousness of the Millions]

Knowing what you now know of microscopic anatomy, you cannot hold to the simple idea that the human body is a single life-unit. This is the na 風e belief that is everywhere current among men today. Inquire among your own friends and acquaintances and you will find that not one in a thousand realizes that he is, to put it jocularly, singularly plural, that he is in fact an assemblage of individuals.

Not only is the living human body as a whole alive, but "every part of it as large as a pin-point is alive, with a separate and independent life all its own; every part of the brain, lungs, heart, muscles, fat and skin." No man ever has or ever can count the number of these parts or cells, some of which are so minute that it would take thousands in a row to reach an inch.

"Feeling" or "consciousness" is the sum total of the feelings and consciousness of millions of cells, just as an orchestral harmony is a composite of the sounds of all the individual instruments.

[Sidenote: Evolution of the Human Organism]

In the ancient dawn of evolution, all the cells of the human body were of the same kind. But Nature is everywhere working out problems of economy and efficiency. And, to meet the necessities of environment, there has gradually come about a parceling out among the different cells of the various tasks that all had been previously called upon to perform for the support of the human institution.

This differentiation in kinds of work has gradually brought about corresponding and appropriate changes of structure in the cells themselves, whereby each has become better fitted to perform its part in the sustenance and growth of the body.

[Sidenote: The Crowd-Man]

When you come to think that these processes of adaptation and heredity in the human body have been going on for countless millions of years, you can readily understand how it is that the human body of today is made up of more than thirty different kinds of cells, each having its special function.

[Sidenote: Functions of Different Human Cells]

We have muscle cells, with long, thin bodies like pea-pods, who devote their lives to the business of contraction; thin, hair-like connective tissue cells, whose office is to form a tough tissue for binding the parts of the body together; bone cells, a trades-union of masons, whose life work it is to select and assimilate salts of lime for the upkeep of the joints and framework; hair, skin, and nail cells, in various shapes and sizes, all devoting themselves to the protection and ornamentation of the body; gland cells, who give their lives, a force of trained chemists, to the abstraction from the blood of those substances that are needed for digestion; blood cells, crowding their way through the arteries, some making regular deliveries of provisions to the other tenants, some soldierly fellows patrolling their beats to repel invading disease germs, some serving as humble scavengers; liver cells engaged in the menial service of living off the waste of other organs and at the same time converting it into such fluids as are required for digestion; windpipe and lung cells, whose heads are covered with stiff hairs, which the cell throughout its life waves incessantly to and fro; and, lastly, and most important and of greatest interest to us, brain and nerve cells, the brain cells constituting altogether the organ of objective intelligence, the instrument through which we are conscious of the external world, and the nerve cells serving as a living telegraph to relay information, from one part of the body to another, with the "swiftness of thought."

Says one writer, referring to the cells of the inner or true skin: "As we look at them arranged there like a row of bricks, let us remember two things: first, that this row is actually in our skin at this moment; and, secondly, that each cell is a living being--it is born, grows, lives, breathes, eats, works, decays and dies. A gay time of it these youngsters have on the very banks of a stream that is bringing down to them every minute stores of fresh air in the round, red corpuscles of the blood, and a constant stream of suitable food in the serum. But it is not all pleasure, for every one of them is hard at work."

[Sidenote: Cell Life After Death]

And again, speaking of the cells that line the air-tubes, he says: "The whole interior, then, of the air-tubes resembles nothing so much as a field of corn swayed by the wind to and fro, the principal sweep, however, being always upwards towards the throat. All particles of dust and dirt inhaled drop on this waving forest of hairs, and are gently passed up and from one to another out of the lungs. When we remember that these hairs commenced waving at our birth, and have never for one second ceased since, and will continue to wave a short time after our death, we are once more filled with wonder at the marvels that surround us on every side."

[Sidenote: Experiments of Dr. Alexis Carrel]

Remarkable confirmatory evidence of the fact that every organ of the body is composed of individual cell intelligences, endowed with an instinctive knowledge of how to perform their special functions, is found in the experiments of Dr. Alexis Carrel, the recipient of the Nobel prize for science for 1912.

Dr. Carrel has taken hearts, stomachs and kidneys out of living animals, and by artificial nourishment has succeeded in keeping them steadily at work digesting foods, and so on, in his laboratory, for months after the death of the bodies from which they were originally taken.

[Sidenote: Man-Federation of Intelligences]

We see, then, that every human body is an exceedingly complex association of units. It is a marvelously correlated and organized community of countless microscopic organisms. It is a sort of cell republic, as to which we may truthfully paraphrase: Life and Union, One and Inseparable.

Every human body is thus made up of countless cellular intelligences, each of which instinctively utilizes ways and means for the performance of its special functions and the reproduction of its kind. These cell intelligences carry on, without the knowledge or volition of our central consciousness--that is to say, subconsciously--the vital operations of the body.

[Sidenote: Creative Power of the Cell]

Under normal conditions, conditions of health, each cell does its work without regard to the operations of its neighbors. But in the event of accident or disease, it is called upon to repair the organism. And in this it shows an energy and intelligence that "savor of creative power." With what promptness and vigor the cells apply themselves to heal a cut or mend a broken bone! In such cases all that the physician can do is to establish outward conditions that will favor the co-operative labors of these tiny intelligences.

The conclusion to be drawn from all this is obvious. For, if every individual and ultimate part of the body is a mind organism, it is very apparent that the body as a whole is peculiarly adapted to control and direction by mental influences.

[Sidenote: Laying the Foundation for Practical Doing]

Do not lose sight of the fact that in proving such control we are laying the foundation for a scientific method of achieving practical success in life, since all human achievement comes about through some form of bodily activity.

We assume now your complete acceptance of the following propositions, based as they are upon facts long since discovered and enunciated in standard scientific works:

a. The whole body is composed of cells, each of which is an intelligent entity endowed with mental powers commensurate with its needs.

b. The fact that every cell in the body is a mind cell shows that the body, by the very nature of its component parts, is peculiarly susceptible to mental influence and control.

To these propositions we now append the following:

c. A further examination of the body reveals a central mental organism, the brain, composed of highly differentiated cells whose intelligence, as in the case of other cells, is commensurate with their functions.

d. It reveals also a physical mechanism, the nervous system, peculiarly adapted to the communication of intelligence between the central governing intelligence and the subordinate cells.

[Sidenote: An Instrument for Mental Dominance]

e. The existence of this mind organism and this mechanism of intercommunication is additional evidence of the control and direction of bodily activities by mental energy.

The facts to follow will not only demonstrate the truth of these propositions, but will disclose the existence within every one of us of a store of mental energies and activities of which we are entirely unconscious.

The brain constitutes the organ of central governing intelligence, and the nerves are the physical means employed in bodily intercommunication.

Brain and nerves are in other words the physical mechanism employed by the mind to dominate the body.

[Sidenote: Gateways of Experience]

Single nerve fibers are fine, thread-like cells. They are so small as to be invisible to the naked eye. Some of them are so minute that it would take twenty thousand of them laid side by side to measure an inch. Every nerve fiber in the human body forms one of a series of connecting links between some central nerve cell in the brain or spinal cord on the one hand and some bodily tissue on the other.

All nerves originating in the brain may be divided into two classes according as they carry currents to the brain or from it. Those carrying currents to the brain are called sensory nerves, or nerves of sensation; those carrying currents from the brain are called motornerves, or nerves of motion.

[Sidenote: Couriers of Action]

Among the sensory nerves are the nerves of consciousness; that is, the nerves whereby we receive sense impressions from the external world. These include the nerves of touch, sight, pain, hearing, temperature, taste and smell. Motor nerves are those that carry messages from the brain and spinal cord on the one hand to the muscles on the other. They are the lines along which flash all orders resulting in bodily movements.

[Sidenote: Nerve Systems]

Another broad division of nerves is into two great nerve systems. There are the cerebro-spinal system and the sympathetic system. The first, the cerebro-spinal system, includes all the nerves of consciousnessand of voluntary action; it includes all nerves running between the brain and spinal cord on the one hand and the voluntary muscles on the other. The second, the sympathetic nerve system, consists of all the nerves of the unconscious or functional life; it therefore includes all nerves running between the brain and sympathetic or involuntary nerve centers on the one hand and the involuntary muscles on the other.

Every bodily movement or function that you can start or stop at will, even to such seemingly unconscious acts as winking, walking, etc., is controlled through the cerebro-spinal system. All other functions of the body, including the great vital processes, such as heart pulsation and digestion, are performed unconsciously, are beyond the direct control of the will, and are governed through the sympathetic nerve system.

[Sidenote: Organs of Consciousness and Subconsciousness]

It is obvious that the cerebro-spinal nerve system is the organ of consciousness, the apparatus through which the mind exercises its conscious and voluntary control over certain functions of the body. It is equally obvious that the sympathetic system is not under the immediate control of consciousness, is not subject to the will, but is dominated by mental influences that act without, or even contrary to, our conscious will and sometimes without our knowledge.

Yet you are not to understand that these two great nerve systems are entirely distinct in their operations. On the contrary, they are in many respects closely related.

Thus, the heart receives nerves from both centers of government, and besides all this is itself the center of groups of nerve cells. The power by which it beats arises from a ganglionic center within the heart itself, so that the heart will continue to beat apart from the body if it be supplied with fresh blood. But the rapidity of the heart's beating is regulated by the cerebro-spinal and sympathetic systems, of which the former tends to retard the beat and the latter tends to accelerate it.

In the same way, your lungs are governed in part by both centers, for you can breathe slowly or rapidly as you will, but you cannot, by any power of your conscious will, stop breathing altogether.

Your interest in the brain and nerve system is confined to such facts as may prove to be of use to you in your study of the mind. These anatomical divisions interest you only as they are identified with conscious mental action on the one hand and unconscious mental action on the other.

It is, therefore, of no use to you to consider the various divisions of the sympathetic nerve system, since the sympathetic nerve system in its entirety belongs to the field of unconscious mental action. It operates without our knowledge and without our will.

[Sidenote: Looking Inside the Skull]

The cerebro-spinal system consists of the spinal cord and the brain. The brain in turn is made up of two principal subdivisions. First, there is the greater or upper brain, called the cerebrum; secondly, there is the lower or smaller brain, called the cerebellum. The cerebrum in turn consists of three parts: the convoluted surface brain, the middlebrain and the lower brain. So that in all we have the surface brain, the middle brain, the lower brain and the cerebellum. All these parts consist of masses of brain cells with connecting nerve fibers.

[Sidenote: Brains Parts and Functions]

And now, as to the functions of these various parts. Beginning at the lowest one and moving upward, we find first that the spinal cordconsists of through lines of nerves running between the brain and the rest of the body. At the same time it contains within itself certain nerve centers that are sufficient for many simple bodily movements. These bodily movements are such as are instinctive or habitual and require no distinct act of the will for their performance. They are mere "reactions," without conscious, volitional impulse.

Moving up one step higher, we find that the cerebellum is the organ of equilibrium, and that it as well as the spinal cord operates independently of the conscious will, for no conscious effort of the will is required to make one reel from dizziness.

As to the divisions of the greater brain or cerebrum, we want you to note that the lower brain serves a double purpose. First, it is the channel through which pass through lines of communication to and from the upper brain and the mid-brain on the one hand and the rest of the body on the other. Secondly, it is itself a central office for the maintenance of certain vital functions, such as lung-breathing, heart-beating, saliva-secreting, swallowing, etc., all involuntary and unconscious in the sense that consciousness is not necessary to their performance.

The next higher division, or mid-brain, is a large region from which the conscious will issues its edicts regulating all voluntary bodily movements. It is also the seat of certain special senses, such as sight.

Lastly, the surface brain, known as the cortex, is the interpretative and reflective center, the abode of memory, intellect and will.

[Sidenote: Drunkenness and Brain Efficiency]

The functions of these various parts are well illustrated by the effects of alcohol upon the mind. If a man takes too much alcohol, its first apparent effect will be to paralyze the higher or cortical center. This leaves the mid-brain without the check-rein of a reflective intellect, and the man will be senselessly hilarious or quarrelsome, jolly or dejected, pugnacious or tearful, and would be ordinarily described as "drunk." If in spite of this he keeps on drinking, the mid-brain soon becomes deadened and ceases to respond, and the cerebellum, the organ of equilibrium, also becomes paralyzed. All voluntary bodily activities must then cease, and he rolls under the table, helpless and "dead" drunk, or in language that is even more graphically appreciative of the physiological effects of alcohol, "paralyzed." However, the deep-seated sympathetic system is still alive. No assault has yet been made upon the vital organs of the body; the heart continues to beat and the lungs to breathe. But suppose that some playful comrade pours still more liquor down the victim's throat. The medulla, or lower brain, then becomes paralyzed, the vital organs cease to act and the man is no longer "dead" drunk. He has become a sacrifice to Bacchus. He is literally and actually dead.

It seems, then, that the surface brain and mid-brain constitute together the organ of consciousness and will. Consciousness and will disappear with the deadening or paralysis of these two organs.

[Sidenote: Secondary Brains]

Yet these two organs constitute but a small proportion of the entire mass of brain and nervous tissue of the body. In addition to these, there are not only the lower brain and the spinal cord and the countless ramifications of motor and sensory nerves throughout the body, but there are also separate nerve-centers or ganglia in every one of the visceral organs of the body. These ganglia have the power to maintain movements in their respective organs. They may in fact be looked upon as little brains developing nerve force and communicating it to the organs.

[Sidenote: Dependence of the Subconscious]

All these automatic parts of the bodily mechanism are dominated by departments of the mind entirely distinct from ordinary consciousness. In fact, ordinary consciousness has no knowledge of their existence excepting what is learned from outward bodily manifestations.

All these different organic ganglia constitute together the sympathetic nerve system, organ of that part of the mind which directs the vital operations of the body in apparent independence of the intelligence commonly called "the mind," an intelligence which acts through the cerebro-spinal system.

Yet this independence is far from being absolute. For, as we have seen, not only is the cerebro-spinal system, which is the organ of consciousness, the abode of all the special senses, such as sight, hearing, etc., and therefore our only source of information of the external world, but many organs of the body are under the joint control of both systems.

So it comes about that these individual intelligences governing different organs of the body, with their intercommunications, are dependent upon consciousness for their knowledge of such facts of the outer world as have a bearing on their individual operations, and they are subject to the influence of consciousness as the medium that interprets these facts.

It is unnecessary for us to go into this matter deeply. It is enough if you clearly understand that, in addition to consciousness, the department of mind that knows and directly deals with the facts of the outer world, there is also a deep-seated and seemingly unconscious department of mind consisting of individual organic intelligences capable of receiving, understanding and acting upon such information as consciousness transmits.

[Sidenote: Unconsciousness and Subconsciousness]

We have spoken of conscious and "seemingly unconscious" departments of the mind. In doing so we have used the word "seemingly" advisedly. Obviously we have no right to apply the term "unconscious" without qualification to an intelligent mentality such as we have described.

"Unconscious" simply means "not conscious." In its common acceptation, it denotes, in fact, an absence of all mental action. It is in no sense descriptive. It is merely negative. Death is unconscious; but unconsciousness is no attribute of a mental state that is living and impellent and constantly manifests its active energy and power in the maintenance of the vital functions of the body.

Hereafter, then, we shall continue to use the term consciousness as descriptive of that part of our mentality which constitutes what is commonly known as the "mind"; while that mental force, which, so far as our animal life is concerned, operates through the sympathetic nerve system, we shall hereafter describe as "subconscious."

[Sidenote: Synthesis of the Man-Machine]

[Sidenote: Subserviency of the Body]

Let us summarize our study of man's physical organism. We have learned that the human body is a confederation of various groups of living cells; that in the earliest stages of man's evolution, these cells were all of the same general type; that as such they were free-living, free-thinking and intelligent organisms as certainly as were those unicellular organisms which had not become members of any group or association; that through the processes of evolution, heredity and adaptation, there has come about in the course of the ages, a subdivision of labor among the cells of our bodies and a consequent differentiation in kind whereby each has become peculiarly fitted for the performance of its allotted functions; that, nevertheless, these cells of the human body are still free-living, intelligent organisms, of which each is endowed with the inherited, instinctive knowledge of all that is essential to the preservation of its own life and the perpetuation of its species within the living body; that, as a part of the specializing economy of the body, there have been evolved brain and nerve cells performing a twofold service--first, constituting the organ of a central governing intelligence with the important business of receiving, classifying, and recording all impressions or messages received through the senses from the outer world, and, second, communicating to the other cells of the body such part of the information so derived as may be appropriate to the functions of each; that finally, as such complex and confederated individuals, each of us possesses a direct, self-conscious knowledge of only a small part of his entire mental equipment; that we have not only a consciousness receiving sense impressions and issuing motor impulses through the cerebro-spinal nervous system, but that we have also a subconsciousness manifesting itself, so far as bodily functions are concerned, in the activity of the vital organs through the sympathetic nerve system; that this subconsciousness is dependent on consciousness for all knowledge of the external world; that, in accordance with the principles of evolution, man as a whole and as a collection of cell organisms, both consciously and unconsciously, is seeking to adapt himself to his external world, his environment; that the human body, both as a whole and as an aggregate of cellular intelligences, is therefore subject in every part and in every function to the influence of the special senses and of the mind of consciousness.

The Supremacy of Consciousness

CHAPTER VI

THE SUPREMACY OF CONSCIOUSNESS

CONCLUSIONS DRAWN FROM STUDIES IN HUMAN PSYCHOLOGY, ANATOMY AND PHYSIOLOGY

[Sidenote: Striking off the Mental Shackles]

Stop a moment and mark the conclusion to which you have come. You have been examining the human body with the scalpel and the microscope of the anatomist and physiologist. In doing so and by watching the bodily organs in operation, you have learned that every part of the body, even to those organs commonly known as involuntary, is ultimately subject to the influence or control of consciousness, that part of the human intelligence which is popularly known as "the mind."

Prior to this, as a matter of direct introspective knowledge, we had come to the conclusion that the influence of the mind over all the organs of the body was one of the most obvious facts of human life.

So, our study of the body as the instrument of the mind has brought us to the same conclusion as did our study of the mind in its relations to the body.

Looked at from the practical science standpoint, the evidences that mental activity can and does produce bodily effects are so clear and numerous as to admit of no dispute.

The world has been slow to acknowledge the mastery of mind over body. This is because the world long persisted in looking at the question from the point of view of the philosopher and religionist. It is because the thought of the world has been hampered by its own definitions of terms.

The spiritualist has been so busy in the pursuit of originating "first" causes, and the materialist has so emphasized the dependence of mind upon physical conditions, that the world has received with skepticism the assertion of the influence of mind over body, and in fact doubted the intuitive evidence of its own consciousness.

[Sidenote: The Awakening of Enlightenment]

The distinction between the two points of view has gradually come to be recognized. Today the fact that the mind may act as a "cause" in relationship with the body is a recognized principle of applied science. The world's deepest thinkers accept its truth. And the interest of enlightened men and women everywhere is directed toward the mind as an agency of undreamed resource for the cure of functional derangements of the body and for the attainment of the highest degree of bodily efficiency.

In some respects it is unfortunate that you should have been compelled to begin these studies in mental efficiency and self-expression with lessons on the relationship between the mind and the body. There is the danger that you may jump at the conclusion that this course has some reference to "mental healing." Please disabuse your mind of any such mistaken idea.

[Sidenote: The Vital Purpose]

Health is a boon. It is not the greatest boon. Health is not life. Health is but a means to life. Life is service. Life is achievement. Health is of value in so far as it contributes to achievement.

Our study of the relation between mind and body at this time has had a deeper, broader and more vital purpose. It is the foundation stone of an educational structure in which we shall show you how the mind may be brought by scientific measures to a certainty and effectiveness of operation far greater than is now common or ordinarily thought possible.

[Sidenote: Your Reservoir of Latent Power]

Remember the two fundamental propositions set forth in this book.

I. All human achievement comes about through some form of bodily activity.

II. All bodily activity is caused, controlled and directed by the mind.

The truth of these propositions must now be obvious to you. You must realize that the mind is the one instrument by which it is possible to achieve anything in life. Your next step must be to learn how to use it.

In succeeding volumes, we shall sound the depths of the reservoir of latent mental power. We shall find the means of tapping its resources. And so we shall come to give you the master key to achievement and teach you how to use it with confidence and with the positive assurance of success._

###